Armed Forces

The War on Terrorism

By John Hamilton

Visit us at
www.abdopub.com

Published by ABDO & Daughters, an imprint of ABDO Publishing Company, 4940 Viking Drive, Suite 622, Edina, Minnesota 55435. Copyright ©2002 by Abdo Consulting Group, Inc. International copyrights reserved in all countries. No part of this book may be reproduced in any form without written permission from the publisher.

Printed in the United States.

Edited by Paul Joseph
Graphic Design: John Hamilton
Cover Design: Mighty Media
Photos: DoD, Preston Keres, AP/Wide World

Library of Congress Cataloging-in-Publication Data

Hamilton, John, 1959-
Armed forces / John Hamilton.
p. cm. — (War on terrorism)
Includes index.
Summary: Reviews the history of the United States armed forces as a whole, as well as of individual branches, and examines the qualifications, training, and activities of twenty-first century Special Forces soldiers.
ISBN 1-57765-674-1
1. United States—Armed Forces—Juvenile literature. [1. United States—Armed Forces. 2. Special Forces (Military science).] I. Title. II. Series.

UA23 .H3642 2002
355'.00973—dc21

2001056668

Second printing 2002

Table of Contents

Rapid Response

A group of U.S. Marines is plucked from the battlefield by a helicopter.

America's Armed Forces

THE UNITED STATES OF AMERICA HAS THE most powerful armed forces in the world today. Its military can strike anywhere, with rapid and devastating results. It has a military tradition that goes back more than 200 years. It has the best-equipped and best-trained soldiers on the planet.

The U.S. is a wealthy country compared to the rest of the world. Wealthy countries can afford large armed forces to protect their homeland. As of May 2001, the U.S. had 1.37 million active-duty soldiers, with almost as many reservists. The U.S. also employs nearly 700,000 civilians who work for the Department of Defense. The defense budget for 2002 was $312 billion. With armed forces that big and well funded, and with the know-how to build and use hi-tech weapons, the United States is a military superpower.

The Department of Defense is the part of the U.S. government in charge of the armed forces. According to the government, "The mission of the Department of Defense is to provide the military forces needed to deter war and to protect the security of our country."

To "deter war" means to build a military that is so strong that other countries won't dare attack—they'll be afraid of being destroyed themselves. When countries go to war, it means that deterrence has failed.

Besides its regular military might, America has a special deterrent used by only a handful of other nations—nuclear weapons. If a country attacks the United States, it must worry that it may disappear under the fire of a nuclear mushroom cloud. Nuclear weapons are a very serious deterrent.

Nuclear weapons are a deterrent against war used by the United States and only a handful of other nations.

Flight Check

A flight crew checks out an Air Force F-14 before takeoff.

The Department of Defense is a cabinet-level organization. The secretary of defense reports directly to the president. The president is a civilian, but he is also the commander in chief of the military. Having the military under the command of civilians is a hallmark of the American government system.

Reporting to the Department of Defense are three military departments: the Army, Navy, and Air Force, plus 15 other smaller defense agencies. The four armed services are under the command of their departments. (The Marine Corps is a second armed service in the Department of the Navy.)

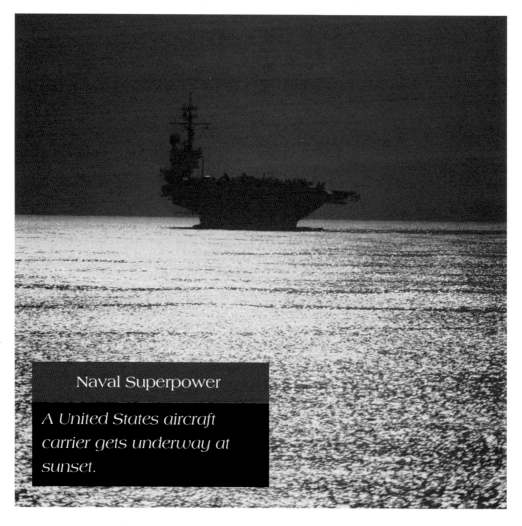

Naval Superpower

A United States aircraft carrier gets underway at sunset.

Each military department is responsible for training and equipping its own forces. In recent years, because of tight budgets, some weapons systems have been developed and used by more than one armed service. This avoids wasting money on needless duplications of hardware and ammo. One example is the new Joint Strike Fighter, a hi-tech aircraft that will be used by the Navy, Marines, and Air Force.

Armed forces exist mainly for self-defense—at least that's what many countries would like to believe. Sometimes countries attack first when they feel threatened. Maybe the threat is real; often it is not. Sometimes countries use their armed forces to threaten neighbors to get what they want. When these threats fail, countries are forced to go to war, often with disastrous results.

Even when wars are started for the right reasons, when evil is fought and conquered, good people die, including innocent civilians caught in the crossfire. The U.S. often tries to minimize civilian deaths by using precision-guided "smart bombs," but they're not perfect. The truth is that war is an ugly business, and people die. It's the job of the U.S. military to be strong enough to keep our enemies from starting a war in the first place. If that fails, the U.S. armed forces aim to finish fighting as quickly and efficiently as possible, while still getting the job done.

A loved one mourns at the grave of a fallen soldier.

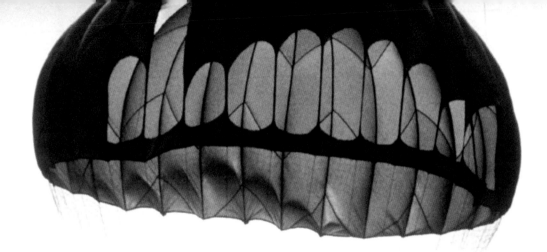

Drop Zone

U.S. Army airborne soldiers parachute into battle.

The U.S. Army

THE UNITED STATES ARMY WAS CREATED during the American Revolution on June 14, 1775. The Continental Congress needed troops to defend Boston, Massachusetts, against invading British soldiers. From its start, the Army relied on citizen soldiers, regular people who give their time—and sometimes their lives—to defend their country. The first American soldiers, the minutemen and the colonial militias, were citizen soldiers. This was unlike many British soldiers at the time. They were paid professionals, sometimes hired from other countries, such as Hessian mercenaries from Prussia.

First commanded by General George Washington, the Army (helped by our French allies) eventually defeated the British at Yorktown, Virginia, and secured the freedoms stated in the Declaration of Independence. The Army helped guarantee the freedoms we enjoy today.

Once America became free from British rule, the Founding Fathers kept the Army to "provide for the common defense," and together with the Navy, to "repel invasion." During the country's early years, the Army was mostly used to defend America's borders and territories.

As the U.S. became a superpower, especially in the past century, the Army has been called on to defend our national interests, often far from America's shores. The Army has fought in 175 military campaigns worldwide since its beginning in 1775. Throughout all those years, the U.S. has used citizen soldiers. Today, the Army has 480,000 soldiers stationed in about 100 countries. Even though they know joining the Army puts them "in harm's way," many people still enlist, eager to fight for liberty. Many have made the ultimate sacrifice by dying for their country.

Infantry

The infantry is the backbone of the Army. When battles rage, foot soldiers are the ones most often in the line of fire. They're the ones who slog through the mud and fight for territory inch by agonizing inch, or defend the homeland to the bitter end.

Being a "grunt" (as they're called in the military) isn't a glamorous job, but no war is won without some kind of force that fights on the ground. Occupying ground and keeping it from the enemy is the infantry's main job.

Even though their protection is weak, today's U.S. infantry is becoming more deadly thanks to hi-tech weapons and communications. Anti-tank rocket launchers, better mines and sensors, more reliable radios, Global Positioning System (GPS) receivers, protective clothing, better food, weapons with increased firepower and laser-guided accuracy—all these things combine to make the infantry a more effective fighting force.

Smokin'

An infantryman races through the smoke during a training exercise.

Armor

The term "mechanized army" basically means troops and guns on wheels. Being mechanized gives an army an important advantage: mobility. Tanks make up one-third of the firepower in the mechanized part of the U.S. Army. The mechanized army also includes trucks for carrying supplies, smaller vehicles such as Humvees, and armored troop carriers.

Tanks are the most fearsome part of the Army's mechanized force. They were originally designed to protect infantry on the battlefield. Tanks still have that function today, but they are also used to destroy the enemy's tanks and other armored vehicles. Today, the U.S. Army relies on the M1A1 Abrams main battle tank for most of its ground combat armor needs.

Tanks cannot gang up and assault the enemy ahead of supporting infantry. Instead, they spend a lot of time hiding from view. Because of their tremendous firepower, they make great targets for enemy anti-tank weapons, such as missiles or mines.

When supported by friendly ground troops who keep enemy troops from sneaking close, tanks make a huge difference in land warfare. Tanks are often called "the arm of decision" because they can be a crucial factor in whether or not a battle is won.

A convoy of tanks during a desert warfare exercise.

Heavy Armor

An M1A1 Abrams, the U.S. Army's main battle tank.

Artillery

Artillery, put simply, uses big guns to lob bombs at the enemy from a great distance. Artillery is an expensive weapon, but it's well worth it. It causes a lot of destruction without exposing ground troops to enemy fire.

Of all the weapons on the battlefield, ground troops fear artillery the most. Artillery bombardment is unpredictable. The enemy is out of sight, and you can't shoot back. Even on today's battlefield, where troops can hide inside armored personnel carriers or other protective cover, artillery barrages can cause morale to plummet. Firing artillery at the enemy can cause them to be frightened and scatter, which makes the infantry's job much easier when the time comes for the main attack.

During World War II, almost 60 percent of all casualties (those killed or wounded) were caused by artillery. Today's U.S. Army uses artillery to support massed ground attacks, most recently

Steel Rain

A 155mm shell is fired from an M-198 howitzer.

during the Persian Gulf War in 1991. In the last 10 years, artillery has improved mainly in ammunition, with the use of sensors and high explosives that better target the enemy.

Most artillery today is self-propelled, with huge guns on tracked vehicles that look like tanks. They can be fired at an enemy many miles away. Today's improved ammunition is very expensive, yet very deadly. Countries that can't afford the newest equipment are at a severe disadvantage when fighting the U.S. Army's artillery.

Self-Propelled Artillery

Mobile artillery hides under camouflage netting.

Air Cav

The old-time cavalry hasn't disappeared—it has simply changed. Unlike the horse-mounted cavalry of yesterday, today's U.S. Army cavalry uses helicopters to strike the enemy, transport troops, and evacuate the wounded.

Helicopters are especially hard for the enemy to shoot. They can flit about on the battlefield at over 100 miles per hour (161 km/h), hiding behind trees and hills, ready to ambush troops or tanks with deadly firepower. Air Cav units can destroy tanks from a distance of almost 20,000 feet (6,096 m) using hi-tech weapons like Hellfire missiles. Hellfires are "fire-and-forget" missiles, which automatically steer themselves toward their targets.

For attacking the enemy, the U.S. Army uses Apache AH-64 Longbow helicopters. Apaches are all-weather helicopters, and they can also attack at night, which makes them especially feared by enemy ground troops.

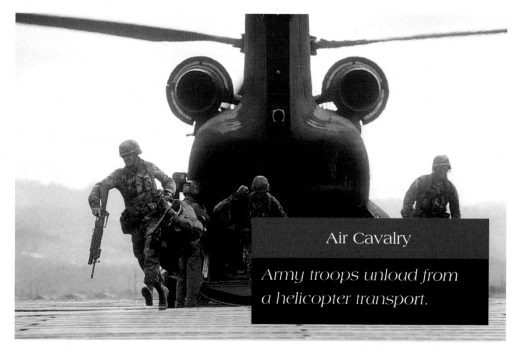

Air Cavalry

Army troops unload from a helicopter transport.

Destruction From Above

A U.S. Army Apache helicopter fires a rocket.

Fury Unleashed

A U.S. Navy battleship fires a salvo.

Victory At Sea: The U.S. Navy

THE UNITED STATES HAS A LONG MARITIME heritage. In October 1775, the Continental Congress voted to outfit two ships with guns and ammunition. These ships soon gave way to the Continental Navy, whose ships were used to fight for independence from the British in the American Revolution.

For the first 120 years of its existence, the U.S. Navy was used mainly to deal with threats to North American shores. Starting in the 1890s and through the end of World War II in 1945, Americans defined their national interests more broadly. The Navy was used to prevent national security threats before they could reach the United States.

Today, the U.S. has national interests worldwide. The earth is 70 percent covered by water, and the majority of its population lives within 200 miles (322 km) of a shore. Because of this, the U.S. Navy is often used as part of a multi-service team to project American power all over the globe.

Even though submarines are becoming more and more important, surface ships are still considered the key part of the world's navies. Modern surface warfare, especially in the U.S. Navy, is carried out with task forces. These are groups of about a dozen ships. Each group consists of one big ship, usually an aircraft carrier, which is escorted by several destroyers, frigates, cruisers, and at least one submarine. The ships travel together, arranged to get the best use from their anti-air, anti-surface, and anti-submarine strengths. A network of supply ships escorts the task forces when they go to sea.

Projecting Power

Navy jets line the deck of a U.S. aircraft carrier.

On Patrol

A U.S. Navy task force sets out to sea.

Naval Air Power

The U.S. Navy first used airplanes for reconnaissance to find out where the enemy was hiding. Naval airplanes still have this role, plus many more. In World War II, the Navy quickly figured out that large battleships were no match for waves of torpedo-launching airplanes. Aircraft carriers soon became the most important ships in the Navy's fleet.

No other country in the world has anything quite like the huge American carriers, which can project power many hundreds of miles away. Carriers like the USS *Theodore Roosevelt* can transport up to 85 aircraft and nearly 6,000 people.

Planes launched from aircraft carriers have many different missions. These include searching for enemy ships and submarines, and striking enemy land targets. In the war in Afghanistan, the U.S. had few airfields close enough to launch air strikes against Taliban and al-Qaeda targets. The U.S. Navy quickly moved several aircraft carriers into position, close enough for strike fighter jets to attack the enemy.

In addition to attacking land targets with aircraft carriers, the U.S. Navy can launch cruise missiles, striking very accurately from a range of about 1,000 miles (1,609 km).

A U.S. Navy jet launches from the deck of an aircraft carrier.

Precision Flying

A squadron of Navy F/A-18 Hornets flies in formation.

Submarines

Submarines are the most feared naval weapons today. Some think they will someday overtake the aircraft carrier in importance, just as the aircraft carrier eclipsed the battleship. The U.S. Navy is unchallenged in undersea warfare, with a fleet of nuclear-powered subs that can attack any target in the world.

Submarines are feared because when they go underwater they are very hard to find. Nuclear-powered subs often stay underwater for weeks at a time. Advanced electronics and sensors help subs detect surface ships, and other subs, from far away. Accurate, long-range torpedoes, cruise missiles, and ballistic nuclear missiles give submarines enough firepower to destroy enemy ships, buildings, or even entire cities.

Run Silent, Run Deep

A U.S. Navy submarine fires a torpedo.

Preparing To Dive

Sailors watch from the conning tower as a U.S. Navy sub cruises on the surface.

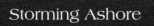

Storming Ashore

U.S. Marines seize a beach during an amphibious assault training exercise.

The U.S. Marine Corps

T HE UNITED STATES MARINE CORPS BEGAN ON November 10, 1775, when the Continental Congress decided the Navy needed highly trained and well-armed troops aboard American vessels. At that time, ships often rammed into each other, and men fought for control of the enemy's vessel.

Today's Marine Corps remains within the Department of the Navy, but it is organized with a great deal of independence. Marines still provide security aboard ships, but their main job today is to seize beaches and naval bases so that U.S. forces can start land warfare against the enemy.

Marines are trained in commando-style warfare, which means raiding the enemy with quick and hard-hitting surprise attacks. Marines, or "leathernecks," as they are sometimes called, are highly skilled and trained. They act as assault troops when invading enemy beaches or ports from the sea. They're the first to go into harm's way to make the beachhead safer for the regular troops who will soon be coming ashore.

To accomplish their missions, the Marines use a variety of special equipment, including amphibious assault vehicles, attack helicopters, and Harrier jump jets. The ability to go airborne means that Marines can invade hostile territory far inland, not just beaches. In the war in Afghanistan, the Marines spearheaded an assault near Kandahar, the Taliban center of power, by first securing a makeshift airfield a short distance from the city. After Kandahar was freed from Taliban control, the Marines then seized the city's main airport, taking it over for use by U.S. forces.

Taking Aim

A Marine sights a target during a live-fire exercise in the desert.

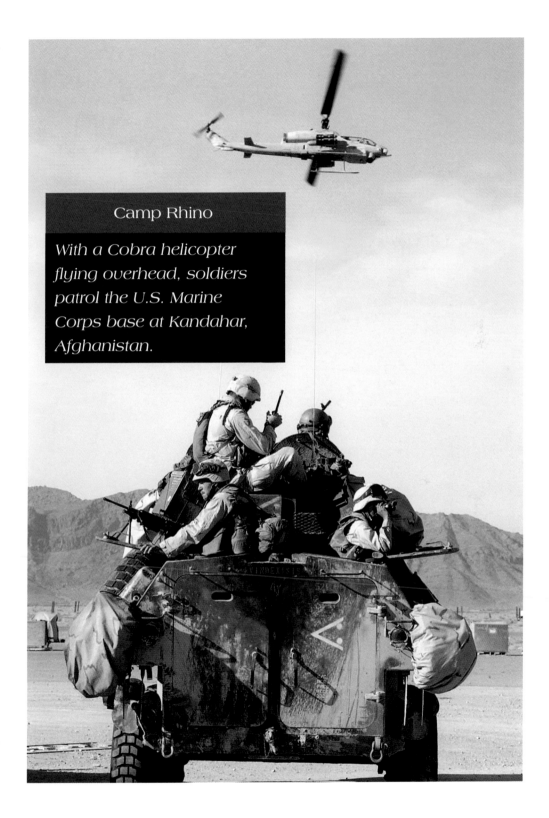

Camp Rhino

With a Cobra helicopter flying overhead, soldiers patrol the U.S. Marine Corps base at Kandahar, Afghanistan.

Soaring Eagles

Two U.S. Air Force F-15 Eagles are put through maneuvers on a combat safety training exercise.

The U.S. Air Force

O N DECEMBER 17, 1903, ORVILLE AND Wilbur Wright made a 12-second flight that changed aviation history, with military history soon to follow. At first, few military planners saw the potential of airplanes in warfare. After their successful use in World War I, however, airplanes were seen as valuable tools on the battlefield. In 1947, after the intense air battles of World War II, the Army Air Service became the U.S. Air Force, independent of the U.S. Army and Navy.

Finding out where the enemy is hiding (reconnaissance) has always been an important job of the U.S. Air Force. Supporting ground troops is another. The reason for the Air Force's increased power on the battlefield today is that it gathers information and uses it better than the enemy. At the modern U.S. Air Force's disposal are detailed maps, improved radar tracking, Global Positioning Systems (GPS), laser-guided bombs and missiles, moving target displays, and a host of other hi-tech electronics. Army, Navy, and Marine aviators also use these advances.

Modern information gathering gives air commanders a very detailed knowledge of the enemy, plus the ability to strike hard and with greater accuracy. By the time ground troops arrive, the enemy's forces are reduced to scattered groups of frightened soldiers. They have been cut off from their commanders and shell-shocked from constant bombardment, often from high-flying aircraft that they can barely see, let alone shoot. It's no wonder that Taliban soldiers in Afghanistan were so eager to surrender.

Eyes in the Sky

Reconnaissance ("recon") missions are flown by experienced pilots with nerves of steel. They fly alone into hostile territory, sometimes fast and low to the ground, to take pictures of the enemy. These photos are used by commanders to make battlefield decisions on whom, when, and where to attack.

Piloted recon flights are not the only information tools the Air Force has available. Robot planes have become more reliable in recent years. In the U.S.-led war on terror in Afghanistan, unmanned Predator and Global Hawk drones were used very effectively to spot the enemy without putting American pilots in danger.

The Predator flies slowly over hostile territory, sending back video images of the enemy. It can stay in the air for 24 hours, and spot objects up to 20 miles (32 km) away. Some Predators have Hellfire missiles mounted under their wings. Operators on the ground can fire these at armored vehicles, such as tanks. In Afghanistan, the Air Force and the Central Intelligence Agency (CIA) used Predator drones to fire missiles at buildings where they suspected top Taliban and al-Qaeda leaders were meeting.

High-Flying Spy

An SR-71 Blackbird spy plane flies high over its target area.

Air Patrol

An Air Force pilot maneuvers his F-15 during a training exercise.

JSTARS (Joint Surveillance and Target Attack Radar System) is a special radar system built into the belly of a Boeing 707-300. Developed jointly by the U.S. Army and the Air Force, JSTARS tracks enemy ground troops and vehicles. For the first time in history, commanders can control a complete battle as it happens. JSTARS data is passed on to commanders on the ground, and to fighter airplanes, which allow for quick and accurate air strikes.

The U.S. Air Force also operates the Air Force Space Command, which is responsible for satellite reconnaissance. These very expensive, high-flying machines can pinpoint enemy positions anywhere on the globe.

Fighters and Bombers

Air-to-air combat is an important part of the U.S. Air Force's mission. By denying the enemy use of the air, it gains uninterrupted reconnaissance ability for its own planes, leaving the enemy without important information. It also takes away the enemy's ability to strike forces on the ground.

Air-to-air fighting has evolved over the years, starting with World War I pilots shooting at each other with pistols and rifles. Today's advanced fighter jets can detect and fire missiles at enemy planes up to 125 miles (201 km) away, though usually missiles are reliably fired at the enemy from a range of 6 to 25 miles (10 to 40 km).

Spotting the enemy first gives an air force a huge advantage in shooting down hostile planes. Roughly 80 percent of air kills happen because an attacker shoots before the defender knows what happened. In this area, the U.S. has a big advantage, with advanced recon electronics giving Air Force pilots the edge they need to strike first.

Strike missions, sometimes called "air-to-mud" missions by pilots, are dangerous and unpredictable. Flying into enemy territory presents all kinds of peril—other planes, anti-aircraft defenses, even the ground itself.

The U.S. Air Force has developed "stealth" aircraft, such as the B-2 bomber, to hide from the enemy. Even regular strike aircraft are equipped with sophisticated electronics to jam enemy radar. And when Air Force pilots do reach their targets, they have a full range of "smart" bombs and missiles that can destroy most targets with very high accuracy.

It has often been said that air power alone can't win a war, that ground troops are always needed to finish the work that air forces start. Over the past 10 years, that idea has been questioned. Air strikes were credited with the majority of victories in the U.S.-led Persian Gulf War, the conflict in Kosovo, and Afghanistan. In Afghanistan, Air Force bombing was especially lethal and effective. The U.S. used friendly Afghan ground troops to capture towns, but by the time they arrived most of the shell-shocked Taliban and al-Qaeda troops were eager to surrender, or had already fled in terror.

U.S. Air Force 1st Lt. Jeannie Flynn, the first female F-15 pilot, performs an engine start.

Bombs Away

An Air Force F-111A drops a payload of Mark 82 bombs over a test range.

Standing Guard

An Army special operations soldier stays alert while on patrol northeast of Kabul, Afghanistan.

Special Ops

I N ADDITION TO THE REGULAR MILITARY, THE U.S. ARMY, Navy, and Air Force include special operations forces. Marines also have special operations units, but they are tightly woven into their regular forces. Special operations soldiers are experts at unconventional warfare. They excel at sneaking into hostile areas and then striking hard and fast. But that is just a small part of what they do.

Special operations soldiers call themselves "the quiet professionals." They are intelligent and highly trained. These elite troops are becoming more and more important in today's warfare.

Special operations forces often use their advanced training and weapons on politically sensitive missions. Only the best-equipped and best-trained troops are used in missions like these, because detection or failure could harm the United States.

Using large masses of ground troops is expensive, dangerous, and time-consuming. An effective option is to use small special operations units to call in attacks from the air. In the conflict in Afghanistan, the U.S. used this kind of warfare very effectively. This helped destroy the ruling Taliban army in less than 10 weeks.

Army Rangers are the U.S. Army's elite light-infantry troops. They are sent on dangerous missions, striking quickly to secure airfields or harbors ahead of regular troops. They are trained to work undetected in harsh terrain—jungles, mountains, even snowy glaciers. Their missions include guerrilla warfare, raids, ambushes, and secretly gathering information about the enemy.

Ranger training is very difficult. Candidates learn to parachute from airplanes, climb mountains in full gear, quickly descend from helicopters, and battle their way out of hostile territory with little food or sleep. Only the strongest (physically and mentally) finish the training.

Rangers who are especially talented and intelligent can move up to a more elite unit, the U.S. Army Special Forces, better known as the Green Berets. These soldiers often work with foreign groups, sometimes in remote and hostile lands. The soldiers train and supply these foreign groups to fight enemies of the United States.

The War Against Drugs

A U.S. Special Forces soldier (right) trains Colombian anti-narcotics troops southwest of Bogota, Colombia.

Unlike other special operations troops, the Green Berets use their brains more than their muscles. (Even so, they are experts with guns, knives, and their bare hands, with combat training similar to Army Rangers.) Depending on where they are assigned, Green Berets become experts at foreign languages and cultures, using their knowledge to train local forces to go on clandestine (secret) missions. While Army Rangers work in large battle groups, the Green Berets use smaller 12-man units called A-Teams. They can operate together without outside help for weeks at a time, gathering information about the enemy or waiting in ambush.

Army Rangers and Green Berets did most of the special operations work during the war in Afghanistan. In addition to working with Afghan resistance forces, special operations troops crept close to Taliban positions and "painted" the enemy with laser beams. U.S. warplanes then dropped "smart bombs," which steered themselves toward the laser targets with great accuracy.

Other special operations units include the U.S. Navy SEALs, who are similar to the Green Berets in combat training, but are especially skilled at underwater missions. The Army runs an elite counter-terrorism unit called the Delta Force, so secret that the Pentagon doesn't officially admit that it exists. The Air Force has its own elite unit, the Air Force Special Operations Command. They are specially trained for search-and-rescue, transport, and close air support, such as firing on targets selected by special operations soldiers, and resupplying special operations units.

None of these units saw as much action in Afghanistan as the Army Rangers or Green Berets—at least not that the Pentagon is admitting. One of the hallmarks of special operations units is that their missions are super-secret. Even when they succeed, the outside world seldom knows about it.

A U.S. Navy SEAL team conducts a room search and clearing operation during a practice ship boarding.

Blending In

A camouflaged special operations soldier prepares to go on a mission.

Where On The Web?

http://www.af.mil/
Official site of the U.S. Air Force. Excellent selection of photos, artwork, and diagrams, plus news stories.

http://www.army.mil/
Official site of the U.S. Army.

http://www.navy.mil/
Official site of the U.S. Navy.

http://www.usmc.mil/
Official site of the U.S. Marine Corps.

http://www.odci.gov/cia/publications/factbook/
Facts and figures about every country, compiled by the United States Central Intelligence Agency (CIA).

http://www.defenselink.mil/pubs/almanac/
Defense Almanac, a site filled with facts and statistics about the United States Department of Defense.

Glossary

casualty
A person who is injured or killed in an act of war.

democracy
A government by the people that is ruled by the majority through representation involving free elections.

early warning radar
Sophisticated radar that detects when enemy planes are entering friendly territory. In war, it is common practice to first destroy early warning radar sites so that the air force can then fly missions with a greater element of surprise.

Pentagon
The huge, five-sided building near Washington, D.C., where the main offices of the Department of Defense are located.

reconnaissance
Finding the location of the enemy. "Recon" missions help commanders decide which forces to send into enemy territory.

smart bomb
A bomb or missile that navigates its way to a target, usually by following a laser beam "painted" on the target by a plane or special operations soldier on the ground. Smart bombs are usually very accurate.

Index

DATE DUE

OCT 1 2002			